THE WORLD HERITAGE

ROMANESQUE ART AND ARCHITECTURE

UNESCO

CHILDRENS PRESS®
CHICAGO

Table of Contents

Library of Congress Cataloging-in-Publication Data
Martin, Ana.
  [Arte romanico. English]
  Romanesque Art and Architecture / by Ana Martin
    p. cm. — (The World heritage)
  Includes index.
    Summary: Discusses the artistic style that developed in Europe between the eleventh and thirteenth centuries, blending Roman art with Germanic and Byzantine elements.
    ISBN 0-516-08387-2
    1. Art, Romanesque—Juvenile literature. 2. Architecture, Romanesque—Juvenile literature. [1. Art, Romanesque. 2. Architecture, Romanesque.] I. Title. II. Series.
N6280.M3313   1993
709'.02'16—dc20

          93-3436
          CIP
          AC

El arte Romanico: © INCAFO S.A./Ediciones S.M./UNESCO 1991
Romanesque Art and Architecture: © Childrens Press; Inc./UNESCO 1993

ISBN (UNESCO) 92-3-102685-2
ISBN (Childrens Press) 0-516-08387-2

3

Romanesque Art and Architecture

In the year A.D. 476, the Ostrogoths, a Germanic people from Central Europe, overthrew the last ruler of the Western Roman Empire. The once vast empire was at an end. Nevertheless, for the next four hundred years, Roman culture survived, thanks to the Christian Church. In a Europe laid waste by war, monasteries preserved the Roman language, art, and way of life. When the conquerors finally settled the former Roman territory and founded their own kingdoms, they made use of this ancient knowledge. Thus they forged the world of medieval Europe, half Roman and half Germanic.

The result of this cultural blend was the artistic style that developed in Europe between the eleventh and thirteenth centuries. It has been called Romanesque—a style inspired by Roman art, with the addition of Byzantine and Germanic elements. Religious pilgrimages and the expansion of monastic orders helped it spread from the Iberian Peninsula (where Spain and Portugal are now) to Scandinavia in northern Europe. Though there were some regional distinctions, the Romanesque style was remarkably similar from one place to another. This style was the first truly European art form, born in an age when Europe was beginning to appear much as it does today.

The Imperial City
Throughout history, Aachen has remained Charlemagne's city. At the end of the eighth century, he turned it into the capital of the first truly European empire. The emperor's tomb and his marble throne are still preserved in the cathedral (top). Below is the interior of the famous Octagon, the cornerstone of this cathedral, which later underwent further construction.

The Carolingian Renaissance

During the ninth century A.D., various artistic styles arose in Europe that are considered forerunners of the Romanesque. The most important of these was the Carolingian style. It developed in Aachen, Germany, in the court of Charlemagne (in Latin, *Carolus Magnus*).

Charlemagne was king of the Franks, a people who lived in the land that is France today. He expanded his kingdom to form an empire that reached from the Baltic Sea to the Mediterranean.

Although he never learned to read or write, Charlemagne admired Roman civilization. He tried to restore the Romans' art, culture, and political system. On Christmas Day in the year 800, Pope Leo III crowned him emperor of the Western Roman Empire. This event marked the close of a time known as the Dark Ages and the beginning of a more peaceful, prosperous era.

During Charlemagne's reign, many great abbeys, or monasteries, were built. Many palaces were built, too, for the emperor and his courtiers. The remains of several of these buildings survive today, such as the Palatine Chapel at Aachen. They show that Carolingian art combined the styles of both Western and Eastern (Byzantine) Roman Empires.

The First Cathedrals

The first great Romanesque cathedrals were built in Germany during the tenth and eleventh centuries. The oldest ones, such as St. Michael of Hildesheim *(left)*, originally had flat, wooden roofs. But at the end of the eleventh century a vaulted roof of stone was used in rebuilding the Cathedral of Speyer *(opposite page, top)*. The cathedral's facade show the influence of the Lombard Romanesque, which was then at its height.

Art for the People

During the Middle Ages thousands of pilgrims crossed the threshold of the Abbey of Vezelay *(opposite page, lower right)* to honor the relics of St. Mary Magdalene. The Biblical scenes that adorned the capitals *(opposite page, lower left)* were created for them. The pictures are easy to understand because they are so expressive — a typically Romanesque feature.

Asturias, or the Art of Survival

One type of Carolingian art was Asturian art. It, too, is considered a forerunner of Romanesque art. When the Muslims invaded the Iberian Peninsula, it was ruled by a people called the Visigoths. After the Muslim conquest, a group of Visigoth nobles and clergymen fled to the mountains of Asturias in northwestern Spain for safety. There they founded a tiny kingdom. After a hundred years, in spite of the odds, the kingdom had not only survived, but expanded. Here Asturian art was born.

Most Asturian churches that survive today were built in the first half of the ninth century. The Holy Chamber (crypt of the ancient Cathedral of Oviedo, Spain) and St. Julian of the Plains (noted for its paintings) both date from the reign of Alfonso II (791-842). But the finest works can be traced to King Ramiro I (842-850). These include St. Mary of Naranco and St. Michael of Lillo, both in the outskirts of Oviedo, and St. Christina of Lena, in the mining town of Pala de Lena. St. Mary was originally the king's pleasure palace, later made into a church.

Asturian art and architecture were the most advanced forerunners of the Romanesque style. Asturians were the first to use huge buttresses against walls to support the weight of vaulted roofs. Over the years, this became one of the most prominent features of Romanesque architecture.

The Asturian Miracle
Only a handful of churches remain as examples of pre-Romanesque Asturian architecture. Among these are the Church of St. Michael of Lillo (top) and St. Christina of Lena (bottom). These churches have a solid profile and buttresses that support the walls. The many ceilings and the stone lattices on the windows are a legacy of the Visigoths.

The First Cathedrals: Hildesheim and Speyer

Charlemagne's empire barely outlasted him. By the middle of the ninth century, it was crumbling in the hands of his descendants. The resulting kingdoms eventually gave rise to the great nations of Europe: France, Germany, and Italy. The first true Romanesque art emerged in Lombardy, in northern Italy, while Charlemagne was still alive. As his empire declined, the Lombard style began to replace the Carolingian. During the tenth century it reached Catalonia, in northeastern Spain. Several churches and monasteries in Catalonia were built in the Lombard style. It spread to Dalmatia and Germany, too.

After Charlemagne's empire dissolved, the title of emperor remained in the hands of German rulers. These rulers also inherited the empire's commitment to art. Like Charlemagne, the Ottos (who reigned during the tenth and eleventh centuries) were outstanding patrons of the arts. But in the tenth century they faced one of the worst moments in European history. Viking, Muslim, and Magyar invaders nearly ended the economic progress that began in the days of Charlemagne. The Ottos fought successfully against the Magyars, who finally converted to Christianity and settled in the land known as Hungary today. To form an alliance with the emperor of the Eastern Roman Empire in this war, Otto I arranged a marriage between his son, Otto II, and a Byzantine princess. This princess, Theophano, was to play a key role in the artistic and political life of her adopted land.

Under the Ottos, new ideas from Lombardy blended with the old Carolingian tradition.

St. Michael of Hildesheim
One of the most interesting figures of the Ottonian period was Bishop Bernwald of Hildesheim. He was born in the middle of the tenth century and died in 1022. He was a highly cultured man who took an interest in all of the arts, especially goldwork. It appears that he was also a notable architect. He was largely responsible for the design of the Church of St. Michael of Hildesheim *(right)*.

The Pilgrim's Goal
The Abbey of Vezelay is sometimes called St. Mary Magdalene, or simply La Madeleine. It played an important role in the history of medieval European religious art. Thanks to the rich donations that wealthy pilgrims made to the abbey, the abbots could hire the finest artists of the day. These artists and architects created magnificent works, such as this thirteenth-century facade *(left)*. Gothic in style, it was restored in the nineteenth century by the French architect Viollet-le-Duc.

LOCATIONS OF
WORLD HERITAGE SITES

The churches and cathedrals from this time were important steps in the development of Romanesque architecture. Shortly after the year 1000, work began in Hildesheim on St. Mary's Cathedral and the Church of St. Michael. Both were started by Bishop Bernwald, tutor to the son of Otto II and Theophano—the future Otto III. Bernwald had traveled to Italy with the emperors and was familiar with classical Roman monuments. Roman influence can be seen in the so-called Column of Trajan and in the great bronze doors of St. Mary's Cathedral. St. Michael's has a symmetrical structure, with an apse at each side. This became a typical feature of the German Romanesque style.

After the Ottos, a new dynasty, the Franconians, claimed the imperial throne. These emperors continued to build great cathedrals. One of the most outstanding of these is the Cathedral of Speyer. In its crypt were buried all of the German emperors from the eleventh to the fourteenth century.

Paintings that Imitate Marble
The Church of St. Savin-sur-Gartempe is most famous for its fresco paintings. Its architecture is also interesting. Around the year 1090, the sanctuary (right) was completed. It is surrounded by an apse aisle and crowned by a narrow cross vault supported by ten columns. A curious painted decoration, imitating veins of marble, covers the shafts of these columns.

Special Terms

apse: part of a church, vaulted and often semicircular, that projects from the rear facade and where the main altar is found.

barrel vault: vault with a circular section and a length greater than its width.

buttress: solid vertical structure that strengthens a wall.

capital: upper portion of a column, composed of moldings and other decorative elements.

cross floor plan: design of a building in the shape of a cross, with the longitudinal (lengthwise) arm longer than the transverse (crosswise) arm.

cross vault: vault created by crossing two barrel vaults.

crossing: space where the central nave of a church crosses the transept.

crypt: level of a church below the main floor.

dome: half-spherical or cone-shaped vault that rises above an open space.

nave: one of the longitudinal spaces that extend down the length of a church.

round or semicircular arch: arch in the shape of a half-circle.

shaft: part of a column between the base and the capital.

transept: the shorter, transverse arm of a cross-plan church.

tympanum: flat surface above the door of a church and below the arch that tops it.

vault: arched ceiling.

At first, the crypt in the Speyer cathedral had a flat wooden roof. But this was replaced late in the eleventh century by a magnificent vaulted roof of stone. Thus Speyer became the first totally cross-vaulted church in Europe. Here the Romanesque style is seen for the first time as a grand and monumental architectural style. Many features of this style were later taken up by the Gothic style, which appeared a few decades after Speyer was completed.

The Growth of Monasteries

Carolingian architecture is seen mainly in palaces. Romanesque architecture, on the other hand, produced monasteries. The style expanded as many new religious orders sprang up in the first centuries of the Middle Ages. It declined as cities arose and monasteries became less important.

Since ancient times, religious communities in the East had separated themselves from the world to live lives dedicated to prayer. This practice, called monasticism, was introduced to Europe by St. Benedict of Nursia shortly after the fall of the Roman Empire. In 529 this monk founded the first Benedictine monastery at Monte Cassino near Rome.

Mausoleum of Emperors
For three hundred years, all of the German emperors of the Franconian dynasty were buried in this crypt of the Cathedral of Speyer (opposite page, top). Considered the greatest crypt preserved in Germany, it consists of three vaulted naves separated by columns. Its only decoration is the alteration of red and white voussoirs, or wedge-shaped stones, in its arches.

Luxurious Artworks
Some beautiful examples of the decorative arts of the Middle Ages are the Cross of Lothario (far right), dated around 900, preserved in Aachen; the stained-glass windows of the Church of St. Savin (near right); and this Gothic sculpture carved in wood at the cloister of the Cathedral of Hildesheim (left).

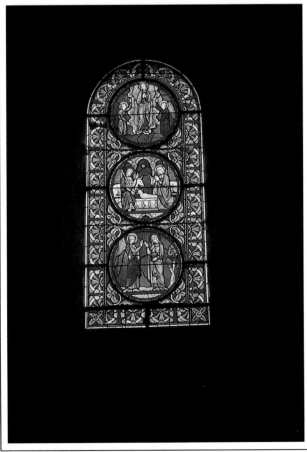

To organize the monastery, Benedict drew up his famous Rule. The Rule called for vows of poverty, obedience, and chastity, and proposed a life based equally on prayer and on work. With a few variations, the Benedictine Rule was adopted by all later orders.

Sixth-century Europe was wasted by famine, epidemics, and warfare. Only the monasteries offered a glimpse of the order and stability that had been lost with the Roman Empire. For this reason, they quickly rose to a high status. They received donations of land, serfs, and jewels. Eventually they grew into great administrative centers, in charge of extensive territories.

Twelfth-century monasteries were very different from St. Benedict's simple communities of barely a dozen monks. The most powerful order were the Clunians, who ruled more than 1500 monasteries. The mother house, in Cluny, France, was a vast collection of buildings, dominated by an enormous and sumptuous Romanesque church. Cluny claimed more than 700 monks and many more laymen, who handled farming and household chores for the abbey.

The monasteries played a leading role in the development of Romanesque art. During the Dark Ages, they were the only places with enough material and human resources to construct great buildings. In following the Romanesque style, they preserved Roman construction techniques while adding new features.

The French Abbeys: Vezelay and Saint-Savin-sur-Gartempe

Many monasteries opened in France, particularly those of the Clunian order. Most French Romanesque churches belonged to great abbeys that have long ago disappeared. On the Hill of Vezelay, in the middle of Burgundy, stands the Basilica of St. Mary Madgalene. It was built in the twelfth century over an earlier Carolingian church. Vezelay was an important pilgrimage center where the relics of St. Mary Magdalene were honored. Thus the abbey became wealthy and powerful. It could hire the best artists of the day when it built its church.

Centers of Wealth and Power
Both St.-Savin-sur-Gartempe *(upper right)* and Vezelay *(lower right)* were once important feudal abbeys that reigned over extensive territories. Each consisted of many buildings, but only their churches survive today. The size and richness of these churches tell much about the power of the medieval monastic orders.

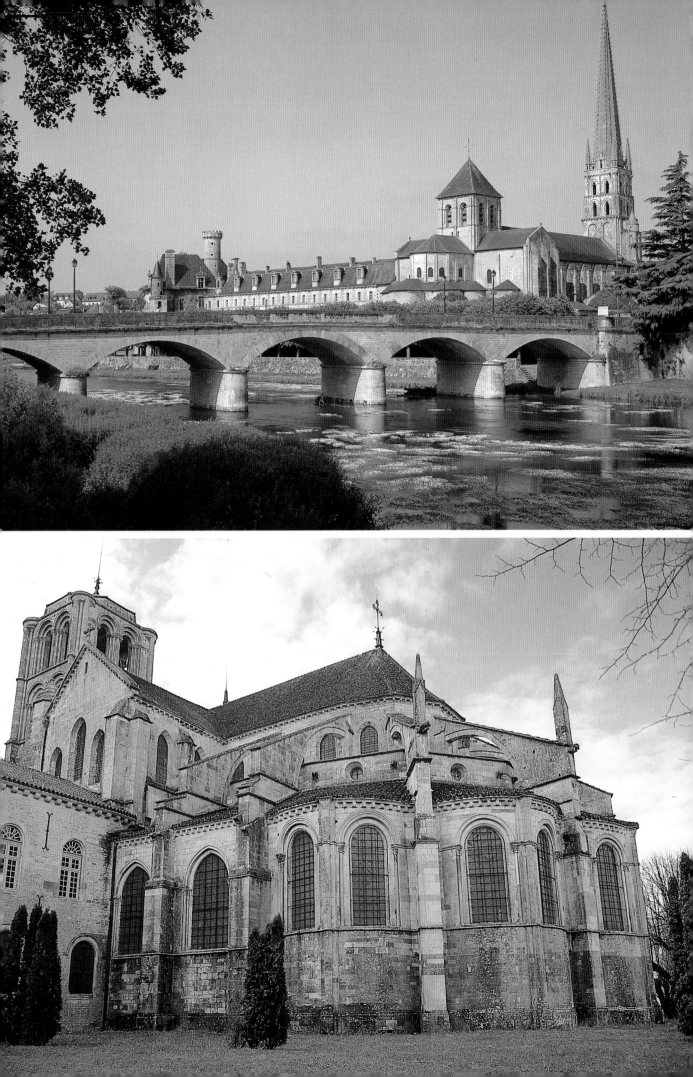

The sculpted decorations of Vezelay are especially magnificent. The main facade, or face, is also outstanding. Its tympanum— above the doorway—depicts the scene of the Pentecost with extraordinary naturalness. In 1146, before this very facade, St. Bernard of Clairvaux preached to the crowd before him of the need to convert the Muslim infidels. This helped inspire the Second Crusade.

Another important French abbey, this one in Poitou, was that of St.-Savin-sur-Gartempe. Founded by Charlemagne himself, it was destroyed by the Normans in 878. Reconstruction began in 1023 and lasted until the twelfth century. The present-day church contains two crypts from the original Carolingian church. The rest is Romanesque, including many paintings. These adorn one of the crypts, the porch, the rostrum, and the vaulted ceiling of the nave. Dating from the twelfth century, they show scenes from the Old Testament, the Resurrection, the Apocalypse, and the life of St. Savin, to whom the church is dedicated.

Features of the Romanesque Style

The Germans were a nomadic people. Thus, they lacked an architectural tradition of their own. Once they needed to erect large buildings, they studied Roman structures throughout the former Roman Empire they had conquered. Thus, Germany's Romanesque architecture follows the Roman tradition very closely.

The most typical Romanesque feature is the replacement of wooden roofs with barrel vaults or cross vaults. Before this time, people knew how to make arched roofs, but used them only in small buildings. Flat wooden beams were still used for the roofs of larger buildings. But Romanesque architecture used higher and grander vaulted roofs than ever before. The walls of Romanesque buildings had to support the tremendous weight of these roofs. So the walls were built especially thick and were reinforced with buttresses against the outer walls.

For the same reason, round Roman columns—crowned with capitals worked in leaf formations—were replaced by solid square pillars. Columns were used in Carolingian architecture, too. Some were brought from old Roman buildings. In St. Michael of Hildesheim, columns and pillars alternate to support the naves.

18

Stone, the Lead Actor
The Romanesque is a solid, heavy style, in which stone plays a leading role. The role of stone can be seen in works from the beginning of the Romanesque period, such as St. Mary of Naranco *(lower right)*, all the way to those in its later period, such as the Cathedral of Speyer *(upper right)*.

19

As the use of vaulted roofs became more widespread, columns were left as little more than a decorative element in windows, porticoes, and galleries.

The Roman heritage is also evident in the use of the semicircular arch. This feature clearly distinguishes Romanesque from later Gothic architecture, which introduces the pointed arch or ogive.

In small decorations, though, we see German and Byzantine tastes. The Germans had their own decorative tradition, based on geometric patterns and intertwined plants and animals. These motifs were used in the decorative arts: goldwork, metalwork, and wood, bone, and ivory carving. Romanesque sculpture and painting were inspired by these models, although Christian themes replaced pagan ones. Byzantine art was also used as a model. Romanesque art shares many features of the Byzantine mosaics in the Italian city of Ravenna: a lack of perspective, well-defined designs, and figures with large, expressive eyes.

Also of Byzantine origin is the cupola, used to emphasize the importance of the transept. Romanesque churches customarily have a floor plan in the shape of a cross. The long arm of the cross is formed by the naves. Usually there are three naves, with the central one taller and wider than the other two. The short arm is the transept. Over the crossing where they meet, it was common to build a cupola. At the front of the church, there are generally one or three semicircular apses.

Pilgrimages and Crusades

During the tenth century, repeated attacks by Normans, Muslims, and Magyars strengthened the practice known as feudalism. Peasants handed their property over to a master and worked the land for him in exchange for the protection of his castle and his army. Thus Europe was divided into a host of tiny states, each organized around a castle and having little communication with the outside. The roads were unsafe, making trade almost nonexistent. Each village lived on what its peasants produced.

After the year 1000, the danger of invasion diminished, and Europe began to prosper once more. Gradually, improved safety on the roads enabled trade to resume, and markets began to spring up. Around them developed towns, whose inhabitants depended on no master. Feudalism began to decline as peasants migrated to these new cities in search of a freer, more prosperous life.

A Crowning Achievement of Romanesque Sculpture
Romanesque sculpture reached its height in Santiago de Compostela with the Portico of Glory (right). The frieze above the tympanum represents the twenty-four old men of the Apocalypse, singing in honor of the Savior. This frieze is an exceptional record of the musical instruments used during the Middle Ages. The picture above shows some of the major elements of Romanesque art.

Who Was Master Mateo?

We know almost nothing of Master Mateo. He is the artist who gave such serene beauty to the faces of the apostles that flank the Portico of Glory. We know only that he was of Galician origin, perhaps the son of Pedro Deustamben, an architect of San Isidro de Leon. It is also known that when he finished his great work he received a lifetime pension by order of the king.

In the matter of religion, people no longer restricted themselves to churches in their own towns. Instead, they set out on pilgrimages to holy places where they could honor relics of the saints. This practice brought visitors and wealth to such monasteries as Vezelay and Canterbury.

The eleventh and especially the twelfth century witnessed the greatest boom in pilgrimages. The three most popular destinations were Rome, Santiago, and Jerusalem. The trip to Jerusalem was particularly difficult, since the city was under Muslim control. This helped to fuel the Crusades—zealous wars to drive the Muslims from Christian holy sites.

The Crusaders failed to achieve their goal, for the Holy Land remained in Christian hands for only one hundred years. But the Crusades played a crucial role in European history. They opened new trade routes, which further stimulated the growth of cities. In addition, they brought a new Eastern influence to European art.

Crypt of the Martyrs
Beneath the apse of the Church of St.-Savin-Sur-Gartempe lies the crypt of St. Savin and St. Cyprian *(right)*. This is all that remains of the original ninth-century Carolingian church. The crypt preserves some interesting twelfth-century paintings of scenes from the lives of the two saints. According to tradition, they were both martyred on this site.

Timeline

476	Overthrow of Romulo Augusto by the Ostrogoths.
529	St. Benedict founds the Benedictine Order.
793	First Viking invasion.
800	Charlemagne is crowned Emperor.
813	Discovery of the Tomb of St. James the Apostle.
848	Consecration of the Church of St. Michael of Lillo.
910	Foundation of the Abbey of Cluny.
1001	Construction begins on St. Michael of Hildesheim.
1023	Reconstruction of St. Savin-sur-Gartempe begins.
1082	Work begins on the new vaulted cathedral of Speyer.
1095	Pope Urban II preaches the First Crusade.
1096	Construction begins on a new church of Mary Magdalene at Vezelay. Destroyed by a fire, it was replaced by the twelfth-century church which still stands today.
1128	The Cathedral of Santiago de Compostela is consecrated.
1135	Gothic reconstruction begins on the Abbey of Saint-Denis.
1168	Construction of the Portico of Glory in Compostela.

The rising cities dealt the monasteries a heavy blow. As universities emerged, the monasteries were no longer the only storehouses of knowledge. Monasteries were also affected by the decline of feudalism. Many monasteries had become powerful landholders. Now, as the monasteries lost power, Romanesque art and architecture also began to fade. Gradually it gave way to the Gothic style.

The first signs of change came, ironically, from a new monastic order: the Cistercians, who were rivals of the Clunians. Founded at the close of the eleventh century, the Cistercian Order attempted to return to the somber simplicity that the Clunians had lost. Cistercian monasteries were the first to employ two typically Gothic features: the pointed arch and the groin vault. The order's success spread these elements throughout Europe. Cistercian strictness, however, dictated that churches must lack ornamentation. For this reason, Cistercian churches cannot be considered truly Gothic.

The true Gothic style began with the renovation of Saint-Denis, near Paris, beginning in 1135. Romanesque churches continued to be built throughout Europe until the thirteenth and even the fourteenth century. But Saint-Denis foreshadowed all of the elements of the great European Gothic cathedrals to come.

A Blend of Styles
The main body of the Church of La Madeleine, or St. Mary Magdalene of Vezelay (right), was completed in 1140. It consists of three naves, one at the center and one on each side. The only decorative elements are the alternating white and dark-brown voussoirs used in the arches which support the central nave. In the background can be seen the apse, built in Gothic style early in the thirteenth century.

The Visigoth Influence
The kings of Asturias thought of themselves as cultural and political descendants of the Visigoth monarchy. For this reason, their pre-Romanesque churches preserve many features of the Visigoth style. In the Church of St. Christina de Lena (left), this influence can be seen in the stone window lattices and Visigoth carvings.

Santiago, Goal of the Pilgrims

The Cathedral of Santiago de Compostela is one of the finest Romanesque churches in Europe. Its magnificent size—and the excellence of the architects and sculptors who created it—reveal the importance of this site during the twelfth century.

In this era, thousands of pilgrims from all over Europe came to honor the remains of the apostle James (Santiago). Along the way there arose a unique variety of Romanesque architecture, culminating in the Basilica of Compostela.

The first church built in Santiago dates to the ninth century. It was built by King Alfonso II shortly after the Apostle's tomb was discovered. It resembled other Asturian churches of the period.

As pilgrimages increased toward the end of the eleventh century, a grander, more sumptuous church was needed. The result was the church which we know today. It was completed in 1128, although some changes were made later.

In 1168 the main portal was replaced by the Portico of Glory. Its creator was Master Mateo, who is named in the inscription beneath the image of the apostle. We know nothing about him, except that he was an exceptional sculptor. Mateo's work represents the height of Romanesque sculpture, in an era when the Gothic style was emerging in nearby France.

The Road to Santiago: Myths and Realities

According to tradition, the apostle James the Great was sent to Christianize the Iberian Peninsula. He crossed the seas in a boat, with only a dog for company, and reached the coast of Galicia. In Padron stands a great stone, or *pedron,* which gave its name to the city. There, it is said, the apostle's boat first touched land.

After preaching throughout the Iberian Peninsula, Santiago returned to Jerusalem, where he was martyred. His devoted disciples gathered up his body and brought it back to Galicia in a boat. The spot where they buried the apostle was later forgotten.

King Ramiro's Pleasure Palace
On the slopes of Mount Naranco, overlooking the city of Oviedo, were the favorite hunting grounds of King Ramiro I. There he ordered a church and a palace to be built. The work was finished in 848, and after the king's death the palace was turned into another church and dedicated to the Virgin Mary. For this reason, St. Mary of Naranco *(right)* resembles the palaces and villas of the late Roman Empire more closely than other Asturian churches.

Another legend tells how the hermit Pelagio, in the year 813, saw strange lights over a place near his refuge. There, in the ruins of an old Roman cemetery, he found a tomb that he identified without hesitation as that of St. James the Apostle. The site was soon known as Compostela, from the Latin words *campus stelae* (field of the star) or *campus apostolae* (field of the apostle). Almost immediately, Compostela became a lure for pilgrims.

Other legends speak of Santiago the Moor-Slayer. Mounted on a white horse, the apostle led Christian forces to victory over the Muslims in the Battle of Clavijo. Thus he was able to free the kingdom of Asturias from the legendary Tribute of the Hundred Damsels, which it had been forced to present each year to the Emir of Cordoba.

During the twelfth century, these legends and many more fascinated thousands of pilgrims who journeyed to Compostela each year. We have a trustworthy account of what this journey was like, thanks to a French cleric named Aymeric Picaud. His guide for pilgrims described the main routes to Santiago, and also provided much practical information necessary for the journey.

Thus we know where inns, bridges, and hospitals were located; on which stretches of the road there was danger from highwaymen; and how much time each stage of the trip required. On the fringes of the legends of James the Apostle, this twelfth-century journey was a living reality that contributed to the evolution of medieval art and commerce.

Art in Hard Times
Such varied monuments as St. Michael of Lillo *(opposite page, left)*, Speyer *(opposite page, lower right)*, Saint-Savin *(upper right)* have a distinct spirit in common. They were created from the fears and hopes of people for whom religion provided the only security, during the difficult centuries of the Middle Ages.

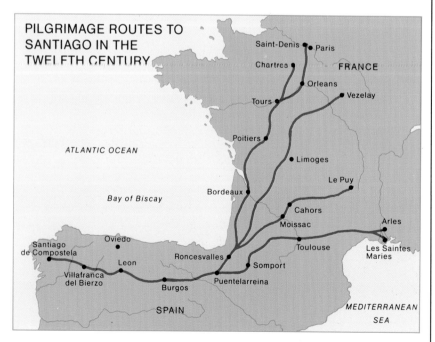

PILGRIMAGE ROUTES TO SANTIAGO IN THE TWELFTH CENTURY

Saint-Denis • Paris
Chartres •
FRANCE
Orleans
Tours • • Vezelay
Poitiers •
ATLANTIC OCEAN
• Limoges
Le Puy
Bordeaux • Cahors
Bay of Biscay
Moissac
Arles
Toulouse
Santiago de Compostela • Oviedo • Les Saintes Maries
Leon Roncesvalles • Somport
Villafranca del Bierzo Puentelarreina
Burgos
SPAIN
MEDITERRANEAN SEA

A Road through Europe
During the twelfth century, pilgrimages to Santiago were controlled by the powerful Clunian Order. Along the four great routes from France to Compostela, Clunian abbeys provided services to the travelers. The journey led to the first great commercial and cultural exchange across Europe.

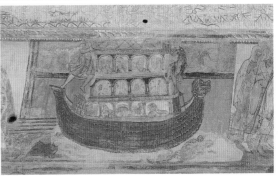

These Sites Are Part of the World Heritage

Cathedral of Aachen (Germany): An outstanding Palatine chapel is the nucleus of the cathedral. Built by Charlemagne at the end of the eighth century, it had an enormous influence upon later European architecture.

Pre-Romanesque Asturian Churches (Spain): These were built in the ninth century by the kings of Asturias, a tiny state in the mountains of northern Spain that remained unconquered by the Moors. Three of them have been declared World Heritage sites: St. Mary of Naranco, St. Michael of Lillo, and St. Christina of Lena.

Cathedral of St. Mary and Church of St. Michael of Hildesheim (Germany): These represent the Ottonian Romanesque style that flourished in Germany in the tenth and eleventh centuries. Both were built by Bishop Bernwald at the beginning of the eleventh century. The paintings on stucco of St. Michael and the bronze doors and columns of the cathedral are outstanding.

Cathedral of Speyer (Germany): The present building dates to an eleventh-century reconstruction by Emperor Henry IV. This was the first fully vaulted church in Europe.

Hill and Basilica of Vezelay (France): On the Hill of Vezelay, where a feudal castle stood, a Clunian abbey was built in the ninth century. The present-day basilica dates from the twelfth century and was completed in the Gothic style.

Church of Saint-Savin-sur-Gartempe (France): On a Carolingian foundation, this church rose during the eleventh and twelfth centuries. It belongs to the Romanesque style typical of Poitou. The most interesting feature is its series of fresco paintings.

Santiago de Compostela (Spain): All of the old section of this city is listed as a World Heritage site. The Romanesque cathedral stands out; it was once the goal of important pilgrimages during the Middle Ages. The Portico of Glory is noteworthy for its carvings, dating from the end of the twelfth century.

Glossary

Byzantine: having to do with the Eastern Roman Empire, or Byzantine Empire, whose capital was the city of Byzantium (present-day Istanbul, Turkey)

courtier: an attendant at a royal court

cupola: a rounded ceiling with a circular base

Dark Ages: a period in European history lasting from about A.D. 476 to about 1000

dynasty: a family of rulers who pass their power down to their children or other relatives

epidemic: a devastating, widespread disease

famine: a period when crops fail, usually due to bad weather or insect pests

hermit: a person who chooses to live in isolation, away from other people, often for religious reasons

infidel: a person with no religious faith or one whose faith is thought to be wrong

medieval: having to do with the Middle Ages, a period in European history lasting from about A.D. 500 to about 1500

monastic order: a community of people who take religious vows and follow religious rules

Muslims: followers of the religion of Islam

nomadic: leading a life of wandering from place to place

peninsula: a piece of land that has water surrounding most of its perimeter

pilgrimage: a long journey to a religious shrine or other holy site

portico: a wide, roofed porch along the front of a building

rostrum: a stage or platform for public speaking

Index

Page numbers in boldface type indicate illustrations.

Titles in the World Heritage Series

The Land of the Pharaohs
The Chinese Empire
Ancient Greece
Prehistoric Rock Art
The Roman Empire
Mayan Civilization
Tropical Rain Forests of Central America
Inca Civilization
Prehistoric Stone Monuments
Romanesque Art and Architecture
Great Animal Refuges
Coral Reefs

Photo Credits

Front Cover: Juan Antonio Fernandez & Covadonga de Noriega/Incafo; p. 3:
J. A. Fernandez/Incafo; p. 5: Michel Escobar & Veronique Hemery/Incafo; p. 6:
Antonio Pradas/Incafo; p. 7: M. Escobar & V. Hemery/Incafo; Kiernan Granger/Incafo;
p. 9: Pepe Abascal/Incafo; p. 10: K. Granger/Incafo; pp. 11–13: Lucio Ruiz Pastor/
Incafo; p. 14: A. Pradas/Incafo; p. 15: M. Escobar & V. Hemery/Incafo; J. A. Fernandez/
Incafo; M. Escobar & V. Hemery/Incafo; p. 17: J. A. Fernandez/Incafo; K. Granger/
Incafo; p. 19: M. Escobar & V. Hemery/Incafo; P. Abascal/Incafo; pp. 21–26:
J. A. Fernandez/Incafo; p. 27: K. Granger/Incafo; p. 29: P. Abascal/Incafo;
J. A. Fernandez/Incafo; P. Abascal/Incafo; p. 31: P. Abascal/Incafo; J. A. Fernandez/
Incafo; M. Escobar & V. Hemery/Incafo; back cover: J. A. Fernandez/Incafo;
P. Abascal/Incafo.

Project Editor, Childrens Press: Ann Heinrichs
Original Text: Ana Martin
Subject Consultant: David Krasnow
Translator: Deborah Kent
Design: Alberto Caffaratto
Cartography: Modesto Arregui
Phototypesetting: Publishers Typesetters, Inc.

UNESCO's World Heritage

The United Nations Educational, Scientific, and Cultural Organization (UNESCO) was founded in 1946. Its purpose is to contribute to world peace by promoting cooperation among nations through education, science, and culture. UNESCO believes that such cooperation leads to universal respect for justice, for the rule of law, and for the basic human rights of all people.

UNESCO's many activities include, for example, combatting illiteracy, developing water resources, educating people on the environment, and promoting human rights.

In 1972, UNESCO established its World Heritage Convention. With members from over 100 nations, this international body works to protect cultural and natural wonders throughout the world. These include significant monuments, archaeological sites, geological formations, and natural landscapes. Such treasures, the Convention believes, are part of a World Heritage that belongs to all people. Thus, their preservation is important to us all.

Specialists on the World Heritage Committee have targeted over 300 sites for preservation. Through technical and financial aid, the international community restores, protects, and preserves these sites for future generations.

Volumes in the *World Heritage* series feature spectacular color photographs of various World Heritage sites and explain their historical, cultural, and scientific importance.